WORKFORCE: BUILDING SUCCESS

TIME MANAGEMENT

Project Consultant

Harriet Diamond
Diamond Associates
Westfield, NJ

Series Reviewers

Nancy Arnold
Metropolitan Adult
Education Program
San Jose, CA

Lou Winn Burns
Booker High School
Sarasota, FL

Jane Westbrook
Weatherford ISD
Community Services
Weatherford, TX

Ronald D. Froman
National Training &
Development Specialists
Winter Springs, FL

Dr. Randy Whitfield
North Carolina Community
College System
Raleigh, NC

STECK-VAUGHN
ELEMENTARY · SECONDARY · ADULT · LIBRARY

A Harcourt Company

www.steck-vaughn.com

Acknowledgments

Steck-Vaughn Company
Executive Editor: Ellen Northcutt
Supervising Editor: Tim Collins
Senior Editor: Julie Higgins
Assistant Art Director: Richard Balsam
Design Manager: Danielle Szabo

Proof Positive/Farrowlyne Associates, Inc.
Program Editorial, Development, Design, and Production

Photo Credits
Cover Photo: © Mark Richards/PhotoEdit
Pp. 4, 5, 6, 12, 13, 14, 22, 23, 30, 31, 36, 38, 39, 45, 47, 53, 54, 60, 62, 63, 68, 69, 70, 77, 78 © From: The ENTER HERE® Series, © 1995 by Enter Here L.L.C.; p. 20 © Bruce Ayres/Tony Stone Images; p. 28 © Mark Segal/Index Stock Photography; p. 44 © Bruce Ayres/Tony Stone Images; p. 52 © Phil Cantor/Index Stock Photography; p. 76 © Phil Cantor/Index Stock Photography.

ISBN 0-8172-6518-X

Contents

To the Learner

Workforce: Building Success is a series of six books designed to help you improve key job skills. You will find many ways to improve your skills, whether you're already working or are preparing to find a job. This book, *Time Management,* is about ways to plan and use your time wisely. To succeed at work, you need to know how to plan and organize your job tasks.

Before you begin the lessons, take the Check What You Know skills inventory, check your answers, and fill out the Preview Chart. There you will see which skills you already know and which you need to practice.

After you finish the last practice page, take the Check What You've Learned inventory, check your answers, and fill out the Review Chart. You'll see what great progress you've made.

Each lesson is followed by four types of exercises:

- The questions in **Comprehension Check** will help you make sure you understood the reading.
- In **Making Connections,** you will read about situations in which people need to use the skills in the reading.
- In the next section, called **Try It Out, Act It Out,** or **Talk It Out,** you will complete an activity that requires you to use the new skills. You might interview someone, conduct a survey, make a telephone call, have a discussion, or role play a situation.
- In **Think and Apply,** you will think about how well you use the skills in your daily life. Then you will decide which skills you want to improve and make a plan to reach your goal.

At the end of the book, you will find a Glossary and an Answer Key. Use the Glossary to look up definitions of key work-related words. Use the Answer Key to check your answers to many of the exercises.

Check What You Know

Check What You Know will give you an idea of the kind of work you will be doing in this book. It will help you know how well you understand time management skills. It will also show you which skills you need to improve.

Read each question. Circle the letter before the answer.

1. Sara works as an exterminator. She uses a truck to visit homes that are spread over a large area. Molly is her dispatcher. How should Molly schedule Sara's appointments?

    a. She should schedule an appointment every hour.

    b. She should look at a map and plan the best route for Sara to take.

    c. She should wait until the morning of the appointments and listen to the traffic report.

2. Manny is part of a crew that cleans up parks. One weekend he finds that he has been given more work than he can possibly do. Manny should

    a. work faster.

    b. decide that it's hopeless and give up.

    c. ask other crew members to assist him.

3. Jane is a nurse in an emergency room. She often does not care for people in the same order in which they arrive. This is because

    a. orderlies don't keep good records of patients' arrival times.

    b. more serious cases must get attention first.

    c. Jane prefers to handle a variety of problems.

4. Pamela works as a personal attendant for an elderly woman, Mrs. Tripp. Mrs. Tripp wants Pamela to run many errands for her. Pamela should

    a. ask a friend to help her.

    b. make a to-do list.

    c. rush to get everything done in one hour.

5. Reggie is taking three classes at the community college. He tends to put off his homework in history, which he finds most

difficult. Now he has a paper due in two days. This shows that Reggie is

a. having a problem with putting things off.
b. prepared to work for one class.
c. able to take day classes.

6. Chi works as a designer. When he starts a new job, he has to stop to find design tools, which takes a long time. What does Chi need to do?

a. gather materials that he will need in advance
b. focus on the new job and ignore distractions
c. make a schedule

7. Jennifer works in a plant nursery. She takes care of the flowers and is usually busy all day. Her supervisor thinks she should be able to get more work done. What might help Jennifer?

a. She should tell her boss that he is a dreamer.
b. She should keep written records showing how much time she takes for her tasks.
c. She should complete her work slowly in the future.

8. Jeff is an ad writer. He often has to refer to old ads that are filed on three different floors in his office building. What Jeff needs to do is to

a. forget about the old ads and do something original.
b. customize his work space to bring his files together in one place.
c. ask his coworkers for new ideas.

9. Alonzo is putting in new plumbing in an office building. One of his tasks requires ten feet of copper pipe, but he has only five feet. The supplier of the pipe is located near Alonzo's house. He should

a. go home for the day.
b. go pick up the pipe and return to complete the job.
c. work on a different project today, and get the pipe on the way to work tomorrow.

10. Dave is a dog trainer. He has many customers, is highly knowledgeable about his work, and is considered very successful. However, he thinks he might want to do some other kind of work. Yet he is not sure what kind of work he would prefer. What should Dave do?

   a. get more customers

   b. study more about different breeds of dogs

   c. take time to consider his long-term goals

Preview Chart

This chart will show you what skills you need to study. Reread each question you missed. Then look at the appropriate lesson of the book for help in understanding the correct answer.

Question Check the questions you missed.	Skill The exercise, like the book, focuses on the skills below.	Lesson Preview what you will learn in this book.
1. _____	Putting things in sequence	1
2. _____	Asking others for help	8
3. _____	Selecting priorities	5
4. _____	Making a to-do list	7
5. _____	Avoiding procrastination	6
6. _____	Planning ahead	2
7. _____	Keeping track of time	4
8. _____	Organizing materials	9
9. _____	Avoiding time wasters	10
10. _____	Examining goals	3

Setting Goals

How often do you set goals?

Are some of your goals more important than others?

Setting goals will help you get more done on the job.

What is a goal? One way to describe a goal is to say it's what you want to do. If you are driving to the grocery store, buying milk is your goal. But there are other types of goals. Goals in the workplace are about getting things done. For example, letter carriers at the post office pack the day's mail in their trucks and deliver it. For letter carriers, delivering the day's mail is the goal.

What does time management have in common with goals? You need to manage your time to accomplish goals. First, identify your goals. Second, put your goals in the best order. If you review your goals carefully, you might decide it is more important to finish one goal than some other goal.

Identify Your Goals

It is important to know your goals and what you need to do to achieve them. Most of your day-to-day goals at work are job assignments. An **assignment** is a job task. You receive assignments from coworkers and supervisors. These tasks are what you need to do in a workday. If you get an assignment from your supervisor, that assignment is your main goal. However, you might set smaller goals that help you complete your assignment. Read the case study below for an example.

Case Study

Tom is a supervisor in a bakery. At the beginning of the morning shift, he plans the day. Tom tells Alex to make 100 loaves of bread by eight o'clock. First, Alex makes sure he understands the assignment. How many loaves? What time does Tom want the bread? Alex writes the assignment down as a reminder.

Next, Alex sets a smaller goal. He will shape twenty loaves of bread every hour. After 30 minutes, Alex has made only eight loaves of bread. Alex knows that he needs to work faster to make 20 loaves of bread in an hour. Because Alex broke his large goal down into a small goal, he is able to check his progress. He can see what he must do in order to achieve his goal.

Every large job task is made up of many small job tasks.

Analyze Large Assignments

In many work situations, assignments are large and complex. Then it's more difficult to set goals. When assignments are complicated, you need to **analyze,** or study, them, before you set goals. To analyze an assignment means to think about the small tasks that make up the large assignment. Use the following questions to analyze a complex job:

- What is my most important goal?
- Which parts of the assignment help me accomplish my main goal?
- Which parts of the assignment make it hard to accomplish my main goal?
- Which part of the assignment should I do first?
- Which part of the assignment takes the longest?
- How much time do I have?
- How much time do I need?

The answers to these questions help you set priorities. **Priorities** are tasks listed in order of importance. Suppose you need to give some information to a client by noon. You also need to complete a report for that client by three o'clock. Calling the client would be your first priority. Finishing your report would be your second priority.

Another skill you can use to analyze jobs is sequencing. When you put things in **sequence**, you arrange steps in the order that you do them. The following case study shows how a team of bakers arranges their tasks in sequence.

Case Study

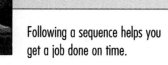

Tanya works at the bakery with Tom and Alex. She and her team are making raisin bread and cinnamon rolls. Tanya analyzes the two goals. They cannot bake the dough unless it has risen first. She plans to have her team work on the rolls first. While the roll dough rises, they will mix up the dough for the raisin bread. While the raisin bread is rising, the team will cut and bake rolls. After the rolls come out of the oven, the bread can go in the oven.

Following a sequence helps you get a job done on time.

Tanya creates a sequence for her two tasks. She needs to divide the baking task into two parts. The dough needs to rise first. Then it can be baked. She could focus on the second task, which is the bread. She identifies her goals and studies them. She also uses sequencing to make plans and meet her goals.

Communicate Your Goals to Your Group

Sometimes you will work with others to meet a group goal. It is important to tell your coworkers about your plans for meeting that goal. Members of your group need to understand the goal and the deadline. The members also need to understand their roles in achieving the goal. Following is a list of ways to communicate group goals:

- **Share information with other group members.** This may mean calling a meeting. It's important to update each other about key issues. If one member of your group is unable to finish his or her work, another member may be able to help.

- **Write a memo.** A memo is a reminder. You can write one memo and give a copy to each member of your group. With memos, everyone continues to understand the group goals.

- **Make checklists.** Group members can check the tasks off as they are completed. A checklist will also give the group a sense of accomplishment. They can see that the goals are being met.

Making checklists is important. After you complete each goal, take time to review what you have accomplished. You need to congratulate yourself. Instead of seeing only endless work, you will be able to see what you have done. If you can be happy about what you have done, you will want to set more goals. As you meet your goals, you will see that you are accomplishing a lot.

Comprehension Check

Complete the following exercises. Refer to the lesson if necessary.

A. Why should you analyze a large assignment?

_____

B. How would you compare an assignment and a goal?

_____

C. Read the following questions. Circle the letter in front of the answer.

1. How do goals help you manage time at work?

   a. When you set goals, you wear a watch.
   b. Setting goals uses time that you could otherwise spend doing something else.
   c. Goals let you know what you need to accomplish in a set amount of time.

2. Tammy feels like she has too many things to do. She makes a list of her goals for the day and then puts a number next to each goal to show how important it is. What skill is Tammy using?

   a. sequencing
   b. setting priorities
   c. communicating

3. Darrel is supervisor of a shop that makes wooden shutters. When he is organizing the work schedule for the day, he is sure to plan for the shutters to be sanded and cleaned before they are painted. What skill is Darrel using?

   a. sequencing
   b. setting priorities
   c. communicating

4. Which of the following is an example of communicating your goals to your group?

   a. writing a letter to a client
   b. putting your tasks in order
   c. writing a memo to three coworkers

Making Connections

Answer the questions following each case. Then talk about your answers with your partner or group.

Case A

Miguel is a teacher's aide. He works in a junior high school. He has several weekly goals. On Fridays, he copies worksheets for the students to do over the weekend. On Tuesdays and Wednesdays, he works with the teacher to make lesson plans for a history class. On Mondays, he corrects homework. On Thursdays, he puts up a display about the history lesson.

Put Miguel's goals in sequence.

First: _____

Second: _____

Third: _____

Fourth: _____

Case B

Rachel is a host at a pancake restaurant. Her boss is Mike. Mike tells Rachel that her most important job is keeping customers happy. On Saturday morning, the restaurant is very busy. People must wait to get tables. Help Rachel to set her priorities. Number the following tasks from the most important to the least important. The most important task should be number 1 and the least important task should be number 4.

_____ operating the cash register for customers who are ready to pay for their meals and leave

_____ helping to clear tables so that more customers can be seated

_____ seating customers who are waiting for a table that has become available

_____ telling jokes to children in line

Case C

Darryl works at a computer store. At the beginning of the workday, Darryl's boss, Mary, tells him to dust off the computers on display, put the boxes of new CD-ROMs on the correct shelves, and move the color printers to another display area. Darryl dusts off the computers. A customer asks him where she can find a book. Darryl takes the customer to the area with the books. Darryl and the customer talk about computer games. Then Darryl unpacks the box of CD-ROMs. Darryl thinks he has finished the most important part of the job task. So, he spends the rest of the morning talking with a coworker. Mary sees Darryl and asks why he hasn't moved the printers.

1. What were Darryl's goals for the morning?

   _____

2. Which goal did he forget?

   _____

3. What skill could help Darryl finish his assignment?

   _____

TRY IT OUT

Talk with someone in your workplace or in your community. Ask how he or she sets goals for a day. Find out if the person you are talking with thinks it's important to set goals. Ask if he or she can tell you about a time he or she needed to set goals but didn't. What happened? Share your findings with the class.

Think and Apply

How well do you use the skills in this lesson? Complete these exercises.

A. Think about what you learned in this lesson and answer the questions. Share your answers with your partner or class.

1. Think about a project you would like to do at home or at work. Maybe you want to paint your kitchen or organize your papers. List smaller goals that will help you accomplish your big goal.

   _____

   _____

2. Think of someone that you know who is well organized. You might think of a friend or a coworker who accomplishes a lot in a day. Interview that person. Does he or she identify goals? Does he or she have priorities?

   _____

   _____

B. Review your responses to A. Complete the checklist. Then answer the questions that follow.

1. Read the list of skills. Check the boxes next to your strengths.
   - ☐ identifying your goals
   - ☐ breaking a big job down into smaller jobs
   - ☐ planning the sequence of your goals
   - ☐ setting priorities for goals
   - ☐ communicating your goals

2. Do you want to improve any of your skills? Which ones?

   _____

3. How do you plan to improve the skills you listed in question 2?

   _____

   _____

Planning

What are some ways that you plan your workday?

How can taking time to plan save you time?

What are some tools that you use to plan?

It takes time to plan your work projects, but, in the long run, planning saves time.

A plan helps you reach a goal on time. If you start a project without a plan, you might make **false starts.** A false start occurs when you do one step of a project and then discover that something else had to be done first. A plan also sets aside time for each task. You will be more successful at work if you figure out the best way to do something before you start a project.

What Is a Good Plan?

A good plan can help you avoid false starts and save you time. A good plan includes each step required to finish a work task. It can also help you avoid problems. Suppose that you need to go to city hall to get a copy of your birth certificate. You could get on the first bus that comes along. However, you might lose time if the bus doesn't go all the way to City Hall. You could plan ahead and check a map of your city's bus routes to find the best way to get there. When you are making a plan, you are thinking ahead. You are drawing a map of how you can get from the start of a project to the finish.

How Can You Prepare for Assignments?

Every worker needs to prepare for the unexpected. A receptionist doesn't know when the phone will ring, but he knows that it will ring. To prepare for calls, the receptionist assembles pens, a message pad and a list of extensions. You, too, can plan for assignments. Planning an assignment includes making sure that you have the **materials** and the **equipment** you will need.

Case Study

Gary is responsible for checking the fire truck. He checks the hoses to make sure they are functioning. He uses a checklist to make sure the radios are working. He also logs all of the equipment and tools. By checking the truck, Gary is learning where to find the equipment that the firefighters will need for a fire. He is preparing for the job of fighting fires.

Before you perform your job assignments, make sure that your equipment works.

Every worker can perform better with a plan. Like Gary, you can take the time to make sure you understand your work project. You can gather your materials and equipment to make sure they are ready.

The following questions can help you to do your planning:

- What materials will I probably need to accomplish my assignments?

- Are all the materials I might need available in my immediate area? If not, do I know where to find them?
- Is my work space clean and uncluttered?

How Can You Budget Your Time?

You are probably used to budgeting your money. You have a limited amount of money to spend on the things that you need. At work, you have a limited amount of time to finish your work task. Planning will help you to use your time in the best possible way. Following are some tips to help you budget your time:

Imagine the finished piece of work to figure out what steps you need to do to complete that work.

- **Visualize.** Think about how your work will look when it is completed. If your work assignment is a report, visualize or picture the pages and the length. Visualize all of the parts that you would like to include. Sometimes you can work backwards from the finished work to figure out what steps you will need to do to complete it.

- **Estimate.** An **estimate** is a guess based on knowledge and experience. Figure out the amount of time you will need to do each task. Then, add extra time to your estimate. If you think a step will take two and a half days, allow three days. You might need that extra time if you run into a problem.

- **Check your progress.** As you do your work, stop now and then. Notice whether your estimates were correct. If you are getting your work done faster than you estimated, then you are ahead of schedule. If you are working more slowly than you estimated, you may need to adjust your plan.

- **Communicate.** Talk with your work team about plans. Your coworkers may know about problems that could come up. They may know of a faster or better way of doing things.

- **Make a schedule.** A schedule is a timetable showing when each step of the project will occur and how long it will take. Use your time estimates to create a schedule. You should share your schedule with other members of your team.

- **Review your plan.** After the project is completed, review it. Study the results. You will build experience as a good planner if you learn from past projects.

These budgeting tips will help you make the most of your time. They will help you finish your work on time. You might even have time left over to seek other goals. The case study below shows how an employee planned a schedule.

Case Study

Maxine works for a construction company. She is planning the work for repairing an apartment complex. Maxine *estimates* how long each step will take. She uses blueprints or designs of the building to help her *visualize* every detail of the project. She finds out when the work crews will be available. Then Maxine makes a *schedule.* Maxine gives a copy of the schedule to each work crew.

Maxine's schedule includes stages or steps to be completed in six months. At the end of the project, she reviews the work. She learns that her plan helped the crew finish the work in four months. With the extra time, the crew can start the next project earlier.

Planning will save you and your coworkers time. It will also save you from last-minute rushes. The next time you have a big project, try to plan first. You might be surprised by how much you can do.

Comprehension Check

Complete the following exercises. Refer to the lesson if necessary.

A. Name one way that making a plan can help you save time.

_____

B. List three skills you should use to help you plan.

1. _____

2. _____

3. _____

C. Read each sentence. Circle the letter in front of the answer.

1. Which of the following is <u>not</u> something a good planner would do?

    a. start working on an assignment without knowing how long it will take

    b. visualize what the product will look like when it is finished

    c. talk to other members of the team about who will do what

2. A schedule should include

    a. a list of the materials you will need to complete the project.

    b. a sketch of the finished product.

    c. a calendar showing when each step will be completed.

3. Reviewing your plan after the project is completed can help you

    a. keep your work space clean.

    b. budget your money.

    c. plan for the next project.

4. Which of the following will <u>not</u> help you budget your time?

    a. making a schedule

    b. giving your work to a coworker

    c. checking your progress

Answer the questions following each case. Then talk about your answers with your partner or group.

Case A

A sales associate in a stationery store needs to plan the displays for the spring merchandise. The displays include everything that appears in the store window. The associate will need to put the products in the window in March. She will make a schedule to help her plan. What should the associate do to prepare for the assignment? What should she use to make a schedule?

_____

_____

_____

Case B

A dispatcher for a plumbing company needs to plan the route of service calls for the plumbers. The dispatcher must tell the plumbers where to go and what to do. Explain how each of the following items or pieces of information could help the dispatcher:

• map

• list of work requests and addresses

• list of plumbers on duty

• knowledge from experience about how long each job will take

_____

_____

_____

_____

_____

_____

Case C

Odessa teaches ballroom dance lessons at a community center. She must plan her classes for the next month. She has a sign-up sheet. Students who signed up for Odessa's class wrote down the days they would be able to come to a class. They also wrote down how much dance experience they already have. How can Odessa use the information on the sign-up sheet to help her plan?

_____

_____

_____

_____

TALK IT OUT

Work with a partner. Find out how many lessons you will study in this course. Then work with your partner to plan your study schedule. Try to schedule the time you will need outside of class to complete the lessons each week. Plan your study time around your work schedule and your personal schedule. Use a calendar to help create the schedule. Then help your partner plan his or her study schedule. Discuss your schedules with the rest of the class.

Think and Apply

How well do you use the skills in this lesson? Complete these exercises.

A. Think about what you learned in this lesson and answer the questions. Share your answers with your partner or class.

1. Think about a project that you recently finished. Name the steps that you did in order to complete the project.

   _____

   _____

2. Make a plan for accomplishing one of your personal goals, such as writing a resume, applying for a job, or learning a new skill. List the materials and equipment you will need. Budget your time. Describe your plan and time budget on the lines below.

   _____

   _____

B. Review your answers to A. Complete the checklist. Then answer the questions that follow.

1. Read the list of skills. Check the boxes next to your strengths.

   ☐ gathering materials that I will need in advance

   ☐ keeping my work area clean and uncluttered

   ☐ visualizing how my project will look when it is done

   ☐ estimating how much time each step will take

   ☐ checking my progress

   ☐ communicating plans to my coworkers

   ☐ making a schedule

   ☐ reviewing the plan

2. Do you want to improve any of your skills? Which ones?

   _____

3. How do you plan to improve the skills you listed in question 2?

   _____

Short-Term and Long-Term Planning

What do you want to accomplish on the job in the next year?

What do you want to accomplish this week?

How do your plans for this week fit into your plans for the next year?

Short-term and long-term planning are the keys to time management.

It has been said that for every minute spent planning, you save three to four minutes in carrying out a job. People who make plans are successful at "getting things done." And, of course, making plans begins with setting goals for the things you want to accomplish.

Most people divide goals into **long-term** and **short-term** goals. Long-term goals are generally what we see in the future and involve needs and wants in major areas of our lives. For a long-term goal, you might ask "Where do I want to be in my career three years from now?" A long-term goal might also be a work task that takes a week or more. Working for such goals may not be on our minds every moment. However, these long-term goals are very important. These goals require careful and exact planning.

Short-term goals involve your day-to-day work tasks. A short-term goal might be "How many checks do I plan to process at work this week?" Short-term goals usually mean simpler plans. In many cases, these goals are easier to fulfill because they are less complex.

Plan for the Long Term

Planning your career is an example of long-term planning. When you plan your career, you are planning for a period that extends far into the future. You might think about your interests and your abilities. What are your basic needs and wants? What are your values and goals? It is first helpful to consider these questions. Then you can start looking for the work you want to do.

A long-term career plan may involve many steps. You might first take an entry-level job and learn the skills you need to advance. You might need education beyond high school before actually beginning your career path. Most career plans stretch across several years. These long-term goals are also personal goals.

Another example of long-term planning could involve your department or team at work. You might have a goal to set up a computer filing system within a year. Or your group might be working on an assignment that will take six months.

Once you set a goal, you can make plans for achieving it. You need to review your resources and time. **Resources** are supplies or talents that you need to complete a task. Resources include materials, equipment, and people. You may need to break your main goal into smaller goals and then decide what you need to meet the goals. The case study on the next page is about setting smaller goals.

Sharon is a teacher's aide in a first-grade class. Her long-term goal is to become an elementary schoolteacher. She set this goal a couple of years ago and gathered information. She learned she would have to go to college to become a teacher. Sharon knew she'd have to work to earn money for college. She decided to work as a teacher's aide because it would prepare her for her long-term goal.

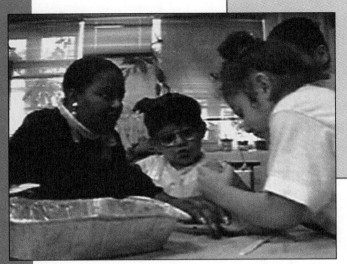

A career goal of becoming a teacher is an example of a long-term goal.

Long-term goals are usually made up of smaller short-term goals. In fact, some long-term goals may seem less difficult if broken down into short-term goals. For example, suppose you work as an electronics technician. You have 60 repair orders for June. Finishing the 60 orders is your long-term goal. To finish each order, you will need to set short-term goals. Getting parts, making the repairs, and running tests to make sure that your repairs have been successful might be some of your short-term goals.

Plan for the Short Term

Long-term plans are made up of many short-term plans. When the short-term plans have all been accomplished, the long-term goal is finished too. Short-term planning also involves resources and time. However, short-term goals are usually more **urgent** or need to be done sooner. Short-term plans are usually used for one day or a week. When you plan for the short term, you must consider every detail of the goal you need to accomplish.

Suppose you sell children's books. Your long-term plan may be to sell a certain number of books in a year. When you plan for the short-term, you might list the stores you need to contact. The following case study shows someone planning for the short term.

Sharon helps plan the morning's activities with the teacher. Sharon makes a schedule. The first 20 minutes of the morning is "circle time," when the class starts the day as a group. Some time must be spent on reading lessons each day. Part of the time will be used for the music class. The last part of the morning before lunch will be ideal for starting a map project she has always wanted the class to do.

Teachers' aides often help teachers plan and schedule day-to-day student activities.

Sharon also considers the supplies she needs. For example, she makes sure the blackboard is erased, and she selects a story for circle time. She gathers the supplies students will need for the map project and plans to set them up while the group is at music class.

Sharon's short-term plans involve deciding on short-term goals. She schedules the amount of time for each activity. With such good planning, Sharon can accomplish her goals.

Make Short-Term and Long-Term Plans Work Together

Sometimes short-term and long-term plans conflict or don't agree. You may have to make a trade-off. A **trade-off** involves giving up one goal in favor of another. Maybe you'd like to start serious training for a marathon in two months. However, a big project at work means working late. Your work goals will cut into the time you have for training. You may have to delay marathon training until the project is done.

Try to plan each day with your long- and short-term goals in mind. Dividing your long-term goals into smaller goals will help. With each small task, be aware that you are making progress. If you plan well, you will accomplish your goals.

Comprehension Check

Complete the following exercises. Refer to the lesson if necessary.

A. List two differences between long-term and short-term goals.

1. _____

2. _____

B. List three steps involved in long-term career planning.

1. _____

2. _____

3. _____

C. Answer the questions. Circle the letter in front of the answer.

1. Which of the following is a difference between short-term goals and long-term goals?

   a. Long-term goals must be done within a month.
   b. Both long-term goals and short-term goals involve planning.
   c. Short-term goals are more urgent than long-term goals.

2. Which of the following is <u>not</u> an example of a resource?

   a. people you work with
   b. trade-offs
   c. equipment

3. Which of the following is <u>not</u> a short-term goal?

   a. completing a package by six o'clock
   b. making a certain number of sales calls by the end of the week
   c. completing a training course for one year

4. Why are short-term plans often easier to fulfill than long-term plans?

   a. Short-term plans are not as complicated.
   b. Short-term plans involve wants and needs in major areas of our lives.
   c. Short-term plans are more fun.

Making Connections

Answer the questions following each case. Then talk about your answers with your partner or group.

Case A

Juanita and Peter want to start their own small moving company. Their long-term plan is to start by moving furniture for homeowners and eventually start a division for businesses. However, before Peter and Juanita can do this, they must set up their business and find some customers.

What might be some of Juanita and Peter's short-term plans?

_____

_____

_____

Case B

Sam, Connie, Erin, and Alicia are members of a team that assembles small electrical motors. Tom has been hired to help Alicia. The first three members are each responsible for putting together a particular part of the motor. Alicia and Tom are responsible for assembling the parts into finished motors. This team is trying to complete eighty motors in two months. To do this, Erin will need to produce more parts per day. Sam and Connie will need to produce more parts per week.

List the short- and long-term goals of this team.

_____

_____

_____

Case C

Allison just started managing the fruit and vegetable department for a new supermarket. She will have to hire several clerks to help her. Her long-term goal is to build the store's fruit and vegetable department into the best in the city. She feels that accomplishing the following goals will lead to her overall goal. Decide whether each goal is a short-term or long-term goal. Write your answer next to each goal.

- making sure that the supermarket's fruit and vegetables are fresher than the ones anywhere else in town

  _____

- unloading boxes of fruit and vegetables that arrive each day

  _____

- offering a wide variety of fruit and vegetables

  _____

- building a network of suppliers with good prices and excellent products

  _____

- arranging fruit and vegetables in the fruit and vegetable bins

  _____

- cleaning the fruit and vegetable display

  _____

TRY IT OUT

Arrange to interview a department manager in a supermarket or other large store. Find out what kinds of long- and short-term goals that person has in the job. Does he or she set any of these goals or are they all prescribed by the store? How does the manager plan to achieve the goals? Do long- and short-term plans ever conflict? If yes, how does the person go about resolving the conflict? Report your findings to the class.

Think and Apply

How well do you use the skills in this lesson? Complete these exercises.

A. Think about what you learned in this lesson and answer the questions. Share your answers with your partner or class.

1. What is one long-term goal you have for yourself? Outline your plan for reaching it.

   Goal: _____

   Plan: _____

2. To accomplish your long-term goal, you must break it up into short-term goals. Refer to question 1. Divide your long-term plan into several short-term plans. List your short-term plans on the lines below.

   _____

   _____

   _____

B. Review your answers to A. Complete the checklist. Then answer the questions that follow.

1. Read the list of skills. Check the boxes next to your strengths.
   - ☐ deciding which goals are long-term and which are short-term
   - ☐ gathering information to help you plan
   - ☐ reviewing your resources
   - ☐ making trade-offs

2. Do you want to improve any of your skills? Which ones?

   _____

3. How do you plan to improve the skills you listed in question 2?

   _____

Focusing

How do you stay focused on your tasks?

What skills can you use to focus better?

The amount of work you can complete depends on your ability to focus.

Staying focused means blocking out everything but your work. It is not always easy to stay focused. You might be interrupted by a coworker. The noises in your work area might be too loud. If you have too much work to do, you might have trouble thinking about a single task. By improving your focusing skills, you can make the most of your time at work.

Understand Different Types of Distractions

You need to be able to concentrate on the tasks assigned to you. That means avoiding **distractions**, which are things that can grab your attention but are usually not related to your work.

Telephone calls and questions from coworkers are common distractions in an office. Loudspeakers and noisy machinery can also take your attention away from work. It is important to know which distractions you can change and which you cannot change. You may be able to move to a quieter work area. However, you will not be able to prevent the phone from ringing. You will need to work with some noises and distractions. Sometimes you will need to respond to these distractions. For example, you might need to stop work on a letter to answer a phone call.

It is up to you to maintain your concentration or focus. Imagine a tunnel that allows you to see only your work. Push out the distractions that you can avoid. You can, however, respond to your coworkers as needed. Set aside time for your hands-on work and time to communicate with others.

Avoid Distractions in Shared Work Areas

If you share work space with a coworker, you may find that there are special kinds of distractions you'll have to avoid. For instance, you may be working in a space where you feel crowded by your coworkers or equipment. Some of your coworkers may be a source of distraction for you. Perhaps they are just friendly and talkative. Some coworkers may bring outside problems to the job with them. How should you respond to these distractions? You can say that you are busy and need to focus on your work tasks. Depending on the situation, you might also want to offer coworkers an option. You can talk to them at a break, over lunch, or after work. You also need to solve your own "off-the-job" problems and not let them distract you at work. The following case study is a good example of avoiding distractions.

Bill works as a sales clerk in a bookstore. One evening, about two hundred customers visit the store to meet an author. Bill is very busy handling customer purchases. Jason, a coworker, begins talking to Bill about the author's new book. Finally, Bill has to explain that he can't talk right now.

"I enjoyed reading the book, and I'd like to hear what you think about it, Jason. But do you think we could talk about this later? I just can't spare a moment now with all these customers at the counter."

Respond politely to a coworker who may be a source of distraction to you.

What do you think of the way Bill responds to Jason? Do you think Bill is polite? Jason asks his question at an inappropriate time, but Bill responds politely. Bill is not distracted by the question. He stays focused on his responsibility, which is taking care of customers.

Identify Your Most Important Tasks

If you have more work than you think you can do, it can be difficult to focus. One way to deal with a big workload is to make a list of job tasks. Suppose you need to complete ten different tasks in two days. You might split up the tasks into two parts. Decide which tasks have to be done first. You do that batch the first day. Then you could do the second batch the second day. When you have a list of your tasks in front of you, it can help you figure out what you need to do first.

You should look at your list often as a reminder. Sometimes your list will need to change. You may not have finished one task yet when your supervisor asks you to work on a different one. Sometimes you will need help from a supervisor to get a clearer idea of what you should do first. Read the case study for an example.

Marcy is the accounts clerk for a small printing plant. She bills the plant's customers during the last week of every month. This month the amount of work seems overwhelming to her. She is having trouble getting started. She decides to talk to her supervisor, Alice.

Marcy says, "We had a big increase in business this past month. I have about twice as many bills to send out this month as I had last month."

Alice responds, "Let's review the bills to make sure we get out the biggest ones first. Then I'll see about getting someone else to help you with this for a few days."

Alice will help Marcy plan her tasks so that the most important ones get taken care of. Also, Alice offers to get someone to help Marcy. Marcy raised this problem in a timely way. As soon as she realizes that she has too much work, she speaks with Alice. The company will get its bills out on time, and Marcy will be relieved of some pressure.

Review the Ways You Spend Time

It's a good idea to keep track of how you are spending your time. A **time sheet** is a record of the amount of time spent on each work task. The sheet looks like a small chart. Sometimes your employer may ask you to keep a written record of your work time. You should keep a copy of the record for yourself. Your records will tell you whether you are using your time well.

Being focused on your job means learning how to avoid distractions. Some of these distractions may come from how your workplace is organized. Some of them may come from coworkers, and some of them may come from yourself. Staying focused will make you a better employee.

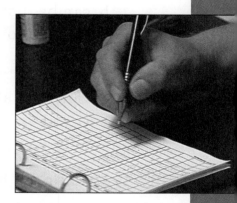

A time sheet is a written record of your work tasks.

Comprehension Check

Complete the following exercises. Refer to the lesson if necessary.

A. What kinds of distractions exist in a typical workplace?

_____

_____

_____

B. How can you be focused and also be alert to your surroundings?

_____

_____

_____

C. Complete each sentence. Circle the letter in front of the answer.

1. Focusing on your tasks means that you have to

   a. block out everything but your work.
   b. ignore telephone calls.
   c. avoid other people.

2. Friendly coworkers

   a. are always not productive.
   b. can be distracting at times.
   c. rely on your help with work.

3. Distractions

   a. call your attention away from work.
   b. can always be stopped.
   c. help you plan.

4. If you need help prioritizing tasks, you should

   a. consult with your supervisor.
   b. get someone else to do the work.
   c. wait until someone offers to help.

Making Connections

Answer the questions following each case. Then talk about your answers with your partner or group.

Case A

Jill works as a legal secretary for two attorneys. Monday morning, each attorney asks her to do some work for them by the end of the week. Jill tries to work on both projects at the same time. By Wednesday afternoon, she reviews what she has done. She is upset because she has not completed much work on either project. As soon as she starts to work on one project, she becomes distracted by the other. She cannot seem to focus.

She asks for a meeting with both attorneys. "Both of you have given me assignments that need to be finished for your court dates," Jill says. "But there is too much work here for me to get it all done by the end of the week."

One of the attorneys responds, "Both of us do need these documents to be ready by Friday. What we should do is call the temporary agency and get someone here today to help with the typing."

The other attorney adds, "Thank you, Jill, for bringing up this problem early so that we could find a solution in time."

1. What problem was Jill facing?

   _____

   _____

2. How did she handle this problem?

   _____

   _____

Case B

Dan is a designer for an advertising firm. He is using a computer to change a photograph of a cat. He has to remove the cat's paw from the photo. The work must be finished by four o'clock this afternoon to meet a printing deadline. His supervisor, George, calls him and wants to discuss the ad that Dan designed for yesterday's paper.

"I like that ad you did for yesterday's issue," says George. "I had some ideas that I wanted to run by you for some of the jobs next week."

Dan knows that George is eager to discuss his ideas now. But if Dan gets involved in talking with him, he will not meet the print deadline.

"I'm glad you liked yesterday's ad," Dan says. "And I'd like to hear your ideas for next week's ads. But right now, I need to focus on finishing the touch-up work on this photo of a cat. We have a press deadline at four o'clock this afternoon."

1. How did Dan express an appreciation for George's comments?

   _____

   _____

2. How did Dan stay focused on meeting his deadline?

   _____

   _____

ACT IT OUT

Work with two people. Take turns being a supervisor, employee, and coworker. Act out the following roles: a demanding supervisor, an employee with too much work, and a chatty coworker. The employee needs to find a way to work with distractions and stay focused on his or her work. When you finish, discuss the ways the employee handled the distractions.

Think and Apply

How well do you use the skills in this lesson? Complete these exercises.

A. Think about what you learned in this lesson and answer the questions. Share your answers with your partner or your class.

1. Think of a place where you worked or studied that had many distractions. List some of them. Were you able to stay focused? Why or why not?

    _____

    _____

2. Think of someone who seems to be able to focus well in spite of distractions. What skills do you think this person uses to stay focused?

    _____

    _____

B. Review your answers to A. Complete the checklist. Then answer the questions that follow.

1. Read the list of skills. Check the boxes that appear next to your strengths.

    ☐ blocking out distractions while working

    ☐ working with talkative coworkers

    ☐ identifying the most important tasks

    ☐ keeping track of how you spend your time

2. Which skills do you want to improve?

    _____

3. How do you plan to improve the skills listed in question 2?

    _____

Adjusting to a Change in Priorities

Have you ever made a great plan and then found out you had to change it?

You may plan your workdays perfectly, but if priorities change, you have to change your plans.

Have you ever rearranged your work plans because your computer was not working? Have you ever had to change plans because someone cancelled an appointment with you? If so, then you changed your plans because of a change in priorities. A **priority** is a goal that is very important. Your first priority is something that you will do before anything else. For example, when you budget your money, your first priority may be paying your rent. When you are making plans to spend money, paying your rent is your first and most important goal.

Put Your Priorities in Order

In the workplace, your priorities are all the assignments that you have to do. When you finish a project, you have one less thing to do. When you get a new assignment, you have one more thing to do. Either way, your priorities change. If you have only one assignment at a time, then every new assignment becomes your first priority. However, if you have more than one assignment at a time, you must decide what to do first. You must determine which assignment should be your first priority. The following list shows ways to put your priorities in order.

- **Find out the deadline for each assignment.** You may want to do assignments in the order in which they must be completed. For example, your first priority could be the assignment that has to be done in an hour. Your second priority could be a task that has to be done by the end of the day.

- **Figure out how long it will take to do each assignment.** Some workers do long assignments first to allow enough time to finish them. Other workers like to do all their short assignments first to make time for large projects. Decide which way of working is best for you.

- **Look at each assignment from your employer's point of view.** What is the main goal of your company? For example, a department store's goal is to sell merchandise. So a salesperson's first priority is usually waiting on customers.

- **Ask your supervisor.** Your supervisor can tell you which assignment should be your first priority if you have questions.

- **Ask yourself, "Is it an emergency?"** During an emergency, you must stop and respond to the emergency. The following case study shows how an emergency can change priorities.

Devon plans to clean the stockroom. He starts to put away boxes. Then a pipe breaks. The stockroom floods. Devon changes his priorities and plan. Instead of sweeping and putting things away, Devon must call a plumber. Devon also prevents the merchandise from being damaged by the water. Before the plumber arrives, Devon moves the merchandise out of the reach of the water. He mops up any water that he can contain.

You may have to adjust your schedule if an emergency arises.

Adjust to Changes

In addition to emergencies, other changes may arise at work that require you to adjust your plans and priorities.

- **When resources change.** A **resource** is a supply or talent you need to complete a task. Your supplies are your materials and equipment. Equipment refers to machinery that you use such as a computer. Your coworkers are also a resource. You may make a plan with certain resources in mind. But if those resources are not available, you have to change your plan. In the workplace, most projects are completed through a team effort. If one of your coworkers can't finish a project, you may need to get more help. If a new person is hired, you may have to allow time to help train that person.

- **When your schedule changes.** A change in deadline can force you to change your priorities. Suppose that an assignment is due sooner than you thought it would be. You will have to find a way to complete the assignment more quickly. You may try to combine some steps. Or, you may divide the work with your coworkers. You may also have to change your plan if you find that the project will take more time than you planned.

Case Study

Maria is a court reporter. She uses a stenograph machine to take notes at meetings and in court. Then she types the notes into word-for-word reports of what everyone said. On Monday morning, Maria plans her schedule for the week. She has a long report that is due Friday. She also has a short report due on Wednesday, so she will type it first. Then Maria finds out that the long report must be finished on Tuesday afternoon. She decides to type the long report first. But she is still worried about finishing her short report on time. So, Maria asks her coworker, Dan, to start typing the short report.

Court reporters schedule time for taking notes in court and typing the reports out of court.

Be Flexible

Employers know that things change. They try to hire employees who are flexible. Being **flexible** means being able to change as situations change. You must also be able to think on your feet. You should be ready to change your plan at a moment's notice.

- **Plan for the unexpected.** Allow for unexpected delays by putting extra time in your schedule.

- **Follow up.** If you change your plan, communicate the change to the coworkers who will be affected. Tell them your new plan. You should continue to keep track of the situation. If your new plan does not work, you may have to change plans again.

Changing plans to meet new situations shows that you are flexible. If you can change plans and still get your work done, you are showing that you can solve problems and stay on task.

Comprehension Check

Complete the following exercises. Refer to the lesson if necessary.

A. Name three ways to decide what assignment you should do first.

1. _____

2. _____

3. _____

B. Complete each sentence using the words from the following list.

coworkers	priorities
emergency	resources
flexible	schedule
priority	supervisor
point of view	

1. Your most important task is your first _____ .

2. A change in _____ might occur when the materials you were going to use are not available.

3. Being _____ allows you to adjust to new situations.

4. If your plans change, you should tell the _____ who will be affected.

5. Your _____ are the assignments you need to do.

6. A(n) _____ can cause a quick change in priorities.

7. To set your priorities, you might consider your employer's _____ .

8. To figure out deadlines, you should ask your _____ .

Making Connections

Answer the questions following each case. Then talk about your answers with your partner or group.

Case A

Jo is a nurse's aide in a hospital. She is responsible for helping the nurses care for patients. Jo is behind schedule for making beds and cleaning rooms. Suddenly, emergency workers rush in with an elderly man on a stretcher. The man is obviously in pain. Do you think that Jo's priorities should change? Why or why not?

_____

_____

_____

Case B

Margo and Tyrone are travel agents. They make arrangements for business travelers. Today Tyrone has called in sick. Margo checks on the travel agency's computer system to find out what Tyrone needed to do today. She discovers that Tyrone is supposed to mail several airplane tickets to a business customer. Margo rearranges her own work schedule. She prepares the airplane tickets herself and mails them to the customer.

1. Why did Margo's priorities change?

   _____

   _____

   _____

2. How does Margo adjust her plan to fit the change in priorities?

   _____

   _____

   _____

Case C

Lauren is a heating and air conditioning technician. She repairs heating and cooling systems. Today she has four different repair jobs. After she completes two jobs, she gets a call from the dispatcher. He tells her that she needs to go to a restaurant to repair a refrigerator. If the restaurant's refrigerator is not repaired by noon, all of the food will spoil. Lauren rearranges the appointments with her two other repair jobs. After Lauren rearranges these appointments, she goes to the restaurant.

1. What type of situation has Lauren responded to?

   _____

   _____

2. How would you describe Lauren's response to the dispatcher's call?

   _____

   _____

TRY IT OUT

Visit a parks department or local YMCA. Interview one of the employees about his or her job. Ask this person how he or she rearranges schedules for activities when factors change. For example, what do the employees do if an activity is scheduled to be outdoors and it rains? How does this employee change priorities and respond to emergencies if someone is hurt? Share your findings with the rest of the class.

Think and Apply

How well do you use the skills in this lesson? Complete these exercises.

A. Think about what you learned in this lesson and answer the questions. Share your answers with your partner or your class.

1. Try to remember a time when you felt as though there weren't enough hours in the day. How did you react to not having enough time? Describe how your priorities changed. Explain how you changed your plan.

   _____

   _____

2. Think of a time you helped a coworker during an emergency. What did you do? How did that affect your own work?

   _____

   _____

B. Review your answers to A. Complete the checklist. Then answer the questions that follow.

1. Read the list of skills. Check the boxes next to your strengths.
   - ☐ finding out deadlines
   - ☐ figuring out how long a task will take
   - ☐ looking at a task from my employer's point of view
   - ☐ putting my priorities in order
   - ☐ adjusting to changes in resources
   - ☐ adjusting to changes in my schedule
   - ☐ figuring out how to change my plan
   - ☐ being flexible

2. Do you want to improve any of your skills? Which ones?

   _____

3. How do you plan to improve the skills you listed in question 2?

   _____

Preventing Procrastination

Do you ever wait until the last minute to do something?

How do you feel if you put off doing something important?

Putting things off can cause serious problems for you and your coworkers.

"Never put off until tomorrow what you can do today." "The early bird gets the worm." Have you ever heard these sayings? They are about avoiding procrastination. **Procrastination** means putting things off until the last minute. If you wait until the last minute to do something important, you may run out of time. You may do a poor job because you're rushed. For example, imagine you are working as a production assistant at a TV station. You are responsible for copying the final cue cards for the announcers. You decide to put off making the cards for the show because you have too many other things to do. The show is about to start and you get started writing them. If you rush to finish them, you might do a poor job. Your procrastination may result in poor work. This lesson will help you avoid procrastinating.

Understand the Reasons for Procrastination

Procrastination is a sign that something is wrong with the way you work. To stop procrastinating, you must figure out *why* you put things off. Here are some reasons why you might procrastinate:

- You have run out of energy. It is hard to do one more thing when you are tired.

- You're not sure how to begin a large project.

- You do not like to do a particular task.

- You are afraid to do a task because you fear you will make a mistake.

- You are in the habit of procrastinating. It seems easier to wait until the last minute than to make a plan.

Read the following case study. Amy works with her supervisor to overcome procrastinating.

Case Study

Amy works for a magazine's accounting department. If payment for an ad is not received, Amy must phone the advertiser. Rita is Amy's supervisor. Rita has noticed that Amy puts off phoning advertisers whose bills have not been paid. Rita talks to Amy about it. Amy is afraid that people will yell at her. Rita and Amy make a plan to solve the problem. When Amy phones an advertiser about an overdue bill, Rita listens to the call. Afterward, Rita discusses the call with Amy. After several calls, Rita offers a few helpful tips. With Rita's help, Amy feels more comfortable. She overcomes her fear.

If you make a plan for completing your work tasks, you will be confident.

Motivate Yourself

The opposite of procrastination is getting things done. The cure for procrastination is motivation. **Motivation** is anything that gets you to act. Think about the times when you feel motivated to do something. For example, if you are crossing the street and a car suddenly races toward you, you feel motivated to jump out of the way. If you read an advertisement for a job that you would like, you probably feel motivated to apply for it.

If you apply for a job, it is because you want to get the job. When you feel motivated to act, it is because you want something to happen as the result of your action. A person that motivates himself or herself is a self-starter. A **self-starter** thinks about what he or she wants to have happen and tries to make it happen. Do you want to get something done? Do you want to learn something new? When you motivate yourself, you are pushing yourself into motion or action.

Keep a Positive Attitude

You will find some tasks more pleasant than others. However, almost any task can also be an opportunity to learn. Perhaps you can show off your skills by completing the task. Ask yourself these questions:

- Does this task allow me to learn something new?
- Does this task allow me to show off my skills?
- Does this task allow me to be creative?

How can you view a difficult task as a chance to be creative? Every workplace and situation will be different, but you can try to find a way to appreciate difficult tasks. Suppose you work as a library assistant. Your supervisor asks you to reshelve the books in a different section of the library. At first, you may be concerned. What if you do not know all of the subjects in that section of the library? What if it takes you too long to complete the work? You could approach this task as a challenge. Perhaps you would create a new system for organizing the books before they are shelved. You might decide to visit that area of the library in your free time to become familiar with it. You can use the opportunity as a chance to show what you can do. Think of new work as a positive experience as often as possible.

Mix Work Tasks

Have you ever postponed work that you dislike? Some people prefer to do their unpleasant work first. Then it's out of the way. You could also switch back and forth between work that you like and work that you dislike. Read the case study below for an example.

Case Study

Dwight is a blood donor technician. Dwight works at a center where people can go to donate blood. Dwight's job is to interview each donor, draw the blood, and fill out the papers that go with the blood donation. He works with two other technicians. Dwight enjoys talking to the donors and making them feel comfortable. But Dwight dislikes paperwork. His coworkers also dislike it because they cannot schedule enough time to complete it. The technicians decide that they will mix up their tasks each day. Each technician will have one hour each day to do paperwork while the other technicians work with donors. These technicians decide to mix paperwork tasks with donor responsibilities each day.

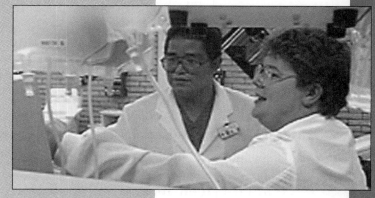

Your coworkers may be able to help you mix your work tasks during the day.

Everyone procrastinates at one time or another. Recognize any tasks that you tend to put off doing. Understand the reasons that you might procrastinate. Then, search for solutions. Mix up your tasks to create the energy you need to perform your job well.

Comprehension Check

Complete the following exercises. Refer to the lesson if necessary.

A. Why do people procrastinate?

_____

_____

_____

B. How can you avoid procrastination?

_____

_____

_____

C. Mark the following statements T (True) or F (False).

_____ 1. The opposite of procrastination is putting things off.

_____ 2. To be a self-starter, you must motivate yourself.

_____ 3. The problem with procrastinating is that you may run out of time.

D. Read the following. Circle the letter in front of the answer.

1. Procrastination is a sign that

   a. you need help from coworkers.
   b. you need to improve the ways you work.
   c. you can handle large projects.

2. You can keep a positive attitude if you try to think of new work as a

   a. challenge.
   b. responsibility.
   c. solution.

Answer the questions following each case. Then talk about your answers with your partner or group.

Case A

Carmen works in a greenhouse. She likes to weed, water, and prune the plants. One of Carmen's duties is to take plants out of pots that are too small and plant them in bigger pots. Moving a plant from a small pot to a big pot is tricky. Carmen must be careful not to break the plant's roots. Whenever Carmen moves a plant, she worries that she will hurt the plant's roots. Carmen puts off doing this task.

1. Why do you think that Carmen puts off moving the plants?

   _____

   _____

   _____

2. What advice would you give Carmen?

   _____

   _____

   _____

Case B

Kenny has a new job in a water treatment plant. Kenny must treat the water with chemicals. Kenny must also figure out how much water to pump into the community every day. These tasks must be done at certain times of the day. However, Kenny has another task that has no deadline. He must check all the equipment in the plant to make sure that it is working correctly. There is so much equipment that Kenny does not know where to start. He put this task off until his boss asked him about it. Kenny is afraid something may go wrong with the equipment before he's checked it.

1. Why do you think that Kenny puts off checking the equipment?

_____

_____

_____

2. What advice would you give Kenny?

_____

_____

Case C

Paulette leads an emergency crew for a gas, light, and power company. Paulette's crew works on water emergencies. If a pipe breaks, they work together to fix the problem. Paulette must keep track of the hours that her crew members work. She does this by entering the hours into a computer. Paulette's plan is to enter the hours in the computer at the end of the day. But usually, Paulette is too tired by the end of the day to work on the computer. Paulette is often in a hurry to do the entries on Friday so her crew can get paid.

1. Why does Paulette put off working on the computer?

_____

_____

2. What advice would you give to Paulette?

_____

_____

TALK IT OUT

Work with a partner. Discuss ways you motivate yourself to do tasks that you don't like.

Think and Apply

How well do you use the skills in this lesson? Complete these exercises.

A. Think about what you learned in this lesson and answer the questions. Share your answers with your partner or your class.

1. Remember an occasion when you waited until the last minute to do something. Did you run out of time because you procrastinated? Why did you procrastinate? Explain.

   _____

   _____

2. Choose a task that you tend to put off. What happens when you put off this task? List two ways to stop procrastinating about it. During the next week, put your plan into action. Explain what happens.

   _____

   _____

B. Review your answers to A. Complete the checklist. Then answer the questions that follow.

1. Read the list of skills. Check the boxes next to your strengths.

   ☐ understanding why I procrastinate

   ☐ motivating myself

   ☐ keeping a positive attitude

   ☐ mixing work tasks

2. Do you want to improve any of your skills? Which ones?

   _____

   _____

3. How do you plan to improve the skills you listed in question 2?

   _____

   _____

Keeping to Schedules

What can you do to get the most out of work time?

Do you sometimes feel you'll never get anything done?

You can be more productive at work if you keep to a schedule.

If you organize your time carefully, you should be able to keep up with all of your work. Keeping to a schedule can make you feel proud that you finished so much work. It reduces your stress, because you know you are on top of things. Most important, when you keep to your schedule, your employer can depend on you. That makes you a valuable employee. Read the following case study to see the importance of schedules.

Case Study

Ray is a home health aide. At 8:30, Ray drives to the home of his first patient. On his way, Ray imagines the day ahead. He plans to see two patients in the morning, attend a class at 1:00, and then go to a laboratory to get blood test results for a patient, Leonard. At the end of the day, Ray will catch up on his paperwork.

Ray's first patient, Ellen, had a hip replaced. Ray checks Ellen's blood pressure and takes her temperature. Ellen likes to talk. She convinces Ray to have a cup of coffee with her. It is 11:00 by the time Ray leaves Ellen's house.

Ray arrives at Antonio's apartment at noon. Ray checks Antonio's chart and discovers that Antonio is scheduled to have blood drawn today. Ray had forgotten all about it. Ray has been putting off refilling his stock of syringes. He is out of syringes, but he can't draw blood without one. He will have to leave, pick up some syringes, and return to draw Antonio's blood later.

Driving back and forth to Antonio's apartment takes Ray several hours. Ray misses his class. After drawing Antonio's blood, Ray drives to the laboratory to drop off the blood sample and get Leonard's test results. By this time, it is 4:30. Ray gets caught in a rush-hour traffic jam. Ray feels frustrated. He doesn't think he will get to his paperwork today.

Home health aides need to stay on schedule to keep their appointments with their patients.

Have you ever had a day like Ray's? If Ray had planned his schedule better, he would have saved himself several hours.

Use Tools to Schedule Your Time

Like many people, Ray felt that he didn't have enough hours in the day to get everything done. To schedule your time, you must plan when you will do each of your tasks. You do not have to organize your time in your head. You can use a calendar, to-do list, schedule, and references to help you.

- A **calendar** shows important information about each day of your week or month. You should write the following things on your calendar:

> important events
>
> meetings
>
> appointments
>
> deadlines (A **deadline** is the day and time that a project must be done.)
>
> holidays
>
> days when people you work with will be out
>
> days when you will be away from work

When you write something down on your calendar, also write down any information you might need. For example, if you must meet someone, write the time, the address, and the phone number in your calendar. That way, all the information that you need is in one place.

If you check off the items on your to-do list as you complete them, you can stay on schedule.

- A **to-do list** is a list of all the tasks you must do. If Ray had put Antonio's blood test on his to-do list, he would not have lost so much time driving back and forth. Organize your list in a way that helps you. For example, you might put a star next to the most important items on the list.

- A **schedule** is your plan to use time to complete tasks. First, check your calendar. Copy events from your calendar onto your schedule. Then, decide when you will do each task on your to-do list. Allow enough time to finish each task.

- A **tickler file** is a file that reminds you to do something. This file is used to keep track of assignments that must be complete by a certain date. To create a tickler file, label a file folder with a date when several different assignments must be finished. Put all the paper related to these assignments in the folder. As you work on the assignments, update the folder. Check the folder regularly to make sure that you are making progress on all the assignments.

- A **reference** is an information tool. Maps, telephone books, and dictionaries are references. They give you information that can save you time. For example, suppose that you must drive to an appointment. First, check a map and plan your route. Then figure out how long the drive will take. Use this information to schedule the time when you must leave for your appointment.

You can also make your own reference tools. Suppose that you need a certain piece of information every day. Don't look the information up every time you need it. Write yourself a note. Post the note where you can see it.

Another information tool you can make for yourself is a **card file** to keep names, addresses, and phone numbers. It may be a physical card file that you keep on your desk. Or it can also be an electronic database that is stored in your computer.

Stay on Track

Create a daily routine that helps you stay on track. Your **routine** is the regular way you do things every day. At work, your routine might include checking your to-do list when you get to work. Update your schedule for the day. Group like activities together. For example, if you must make several phone calls, plan to make them one right after the other at a certain time. Stick to your to-do list. When you finish a task, cross it off your to-do list. Change your schedule if you are interrupted. If you must do something that you didn't know you would have to do, adjust your schedule. Reschedule some tasks. At the end of the day, make your to-do list for the next day.

Comprehension Check

Complete the following exercises. Refer to the lesson if necessary.

A. Name two tools you can use to organize your time.

1. _____

2. _____

B. Name three steps that can help you stay on track if you include them in your daily routine.

1. _____

2. _____

3. _____

C. Match the definition in the first column with the correct word or phrase in the second column. Write the letter of the correct word.

_____ 1. a tool you can use to plan your week or month

_____ 2. a way you can stay on track during your day

_____ 3. a tool you can use to remind you of tasks

_____ 4. a card file of addresses and phone numbers

_____ 5. a tool you can use to find information

_____ 6. a file of assignments arranged by date

_____ 7. an item you might include on a calendar

a. create a routine
b. to-do list
c. calendar
d. reference materials
e. card file
f. tickler file
g. meeting

Answer the questions following each case. Then talk about your answers with your partner or group.

Case A

Maureen is a truck driver. One morning, Maureen picks up a list of the deliveries she must make. She gets her truck, which is already loaded. Then, she climbs in her truck and drives away to make the deliveries. As she is driving, Maureen hears a thud. She looks in her rear-view mirror and sees that a box has fallen out of the back of the truck. Maureen pulls over and goes to get the box. While she is pulled over, Maureen checks her list of deliveries. She realizes that she has started to drive in the wrong direction. She had to go this way yesterday, but today her first delivery is on the other side of town. Maureen turns around and heads for her first stop. On the way, she runs out of gas. She will probably be late with her deliveries.

What could Maureen have done to stay on track?

_____

_____

Case B

David is a reporter for a newspaper. He needs to report on a story at the police station. He looks at a map to find his way there. After arriving, he takes notes of what the officers say. He tape records the statements made by each person. He returns to his office to type the statements and write the story. He also looks at a dictionary to correct his spelling. His deadline is at ten o'clock on Friday.

What tools do you think that David uses to control his time?

_____

_____

Case C

Bill is the Chicago dispatcher for Express-O, an overnight delivery service. Elizabeth phones Bill late one evening. She wants to send a package from Chicago to Houston. The package must arrive in Houston by 10:00 a.m. Bill sends someone to pick up Elizabeth's package. Then, Bill must figure out how to get the package delivered on time. His computer can show him the travel schedule for Express-O trucks and planes. It can also show him a map of their routes. Bill's computer can even show him weather maps for anyplace in the world. What do you think that Bill should do?

_____

_____

TRY IT OUT

Go to a local office supply store. Make a list of the time management tools you find there. What are they used for? Ask a salesperson which time management tools sell the best. What are they used for and why? Are there any time management tools you want to use? Report your findings to the class.

Think and Apply

How well do you use the skills in this lesson? Complete these exercises.

A. Think about what you learned in this lesson and answer the questions. Share your answers with your partner or your class.

1. Think of a time when you believed that you didn't have time to do everything that you needed to do. What happened? Would you do anything differently now?

   _____

2. Plan your schedule for the next week. Make a to-do list. Write each task on your calendar on the day that you plan to do it. (If you do not have a calendar, you can draw one for the week. Just draw a box for each day.) Check your calendar every day. Did you do everything on your to-do list? Why or why not? How could you improve?

   _____

B. Review your answers to A. Complete the checklist. Then answer the questions that follow.

1. Read the list of skills. Check the boxes next to your strengths.
   - ☐ using a calendar
   - ☐ making a to-do list
   - ☐ making a schedule
   - ☐ using a tickler file
   - ☐ getting information from references
   - ☐ using a routine to stay on track

2. Do you want to improve any of your skills? Which ones?

   _____

3. How do you plan to improve the skills you listed in question 2?

   _____

Managing Time During a Crisis

What happens when you have too much to do?

How do you deal with too much stress?

How do you complete your work?

A crisis tests your time management skills.

Have you ever started a project, thinking that it would only take a few minutes, and then discovered that it would take you several hours? Have you ever had to do your own work, plus the work of a coworker who called in sick? When you have more work than you can possibly finish, you are in a **crisis**. In a crisis, you have two problems. The first problem is that you feel stress. The second problem is that you must somehow finish your work. You can solve both of these problems by managing your time carefully. First, you must lower your stress because stress can prevent you from managing your time wisely.

Lower Your Stress

Stress occurs when you feel tense about a situation. Lowering your stress will allow you to focus on your work and begin to make progress. There are techniques that can lower your stress. Take a minute to take deep breaths. Breathe in slowly. Then breathe out slowly. Breathing deeply provides more oxygen to your brain. When your brain has plenty of oxygen, you have more energy and it is easier for you to concentrate. You are more likely to do a task well if you give it your full attention. Also don't let your emotions take over. Focus on how to get each task done. Read the following case study to see how to handle stress.

Case Study

Vada runs a printing press. Today, she must print a color catalog and several posters. Vada feels stress because color catalogs take a long time to print. Vada is afraid that she may not get everything done. Vada decides that in order to do her work, she will have to calm down. She stops what she is doing and takes several deep breaths. Once she has dealt with her emotions, Vada's mind is clear. Now she is ready to figure out how to meet her deadlines.

Make Decisions

Most people have avoided making a tough decision at one time or another. Making a decision means taking responsibility for your actions. Making decisions requires courage. This can be scary. But to deal with a crisis, you often must make decisions quickly. If you take too long to make a decision, you will lose time. Use the following tips to help you see past the crisis to a solution.

Gather information. Gather all the facts you will need. Gathering information may include asking questions. You can also gather information in other ways, depending on the crisis. For example, if your crisis involves the use of a computer, you might check the computer manual for information.

List pros and cons. In a crisis, consider at least three solutions. Then list the "pros" or positives and the "cons" or negatives for each solution. Then, if you have more pros than cons for one solution, that decision is probably the best one. For example, suppose that you are about to help a customer. Your phone starts ringing. You must quickly weigh the pros and cons of answering the phone. The pros might be that the phone would stop ringing and the caller would be pleased at not having to wait. The con is that the customer you were about to help must wait while you answer the phone.

Rate your decisions. Rate your decisions from one to ten. One is the least attractive solution and ten is the most attractive. In some cases, you may have to make a decision that rates as a five. It is not an ideal solution, but it is the best you can do under the circumstances.

Ask questions to gather the information you need to make decisions.

Working Effectively During a Crisis

In a crisis, you need to figure out a more effective way to do things. **Effective** means producing a desired result or end. Here are some techniques you can use to work effectively.

Arrange the steps of each task. You should try to find the best order in which to do your tasks. For example, if you must drive to several different places, it makes sense to drive to the closest place first.

Group tasks together. If the same step is part of more than one task, do that step only once. For example, wait until you've finished all of the letters you need to send out for the day before you go to the mailroom.

Use downtime. **Downtime** is any time when work is getting done, but you are not doing it. An office worker has downtime when a long document is printing. A restaurant worker has downtime when coffee is dripping from the coffee machine into the pot. Use downtime to do something else. For example, a restaurant worker can wait on customers while the coffee machine is making coffee. Start tasks that include downtime early. Then, do short tasks during the downtime from long tasks.

Delegate. Teamwork is important in a crisis. Ask your supervisor if you may get help from your coworkers. Then, ask your coworkers if they have time to help you. When you give some of your work to a coworker, you are **delegating**. Delegate tasks that require as little explanation as possible. The following case study shows how delegating helps in a crisis.

People who work in food service jobs often delegate tasks to manage their time.

Case Study

Mario, Francois, and Lessa cook for a restaurant. The cooks are short-staffed today because Camille, another cook, burned her hand. She had to go home. Mario has pasta cooking in one pot and sauce cooking in another. Mario is also chopping ingredients. The three cooks work as a team to get the work done. When Lessa goes to the cooler, Mario asks her to bring something back that he needs, too. When Francois has a minute, Mario asks Francois to stir the sauce. The cooks save time by delegating.

A crisis may last just a few hours or all day. In a short crisis, you might only spend a few seconds planning how to deal with it. In a long crisis, you might need more planning time. No matter how long the crisis lasts, you can use the same skills to deal with it.

Comprehension Check

Complete the following exercises. Refer to the lesson if necessary.

A. Name two ways to lower your stress.

1. _____

2. _____

B. What is downtime, and how can you use it to work effectively in a crisis?

_____

_____

C. Complete each sentence using words from the following list.

courage   group tasks
crisis   pros and cons
information   stress
delegating

1. Lowering your _____ helps you focus on your work.

2. When you have too much work and not enough time, you are in a _____ .

3. Making decisions requires _____ .

4. Asking questions is one way to gather _____ .

5. When you give some of your work to a coworker, you are _____ .

6. If you need to perform the same task more than once, you could _____ to work more efficiently.

7. Listing the positives and negatives of a solution is called listing the _____ .

Making Connections

Answer the questions following each case. Then talk about your answers with your partner or group.

Case A

Peter and Vanessa are flight attendants. Their job is to make sure that the passengers on an airplane are comfortable and safe. They also serve refreshments. Today, they are on a short flight. Vanessa makes an announcement advising the passengers that they should keep their seat belts fastened because the flight may be bumpy. Peter wheels a cart down the center of the plane. He must serve drinks to everyone. Peter feels stressed because he only has 20 minutes to serve the drinks and pick them up again. Then, two different passengers try to get Peter's attention. One passenger asks Peter for a magazine. The other passenger feels sick and wants an airsickness bag. Peter feels that he has too much to do and not enough time to do it in. Name one thing Peter can do to deal with this crisis.

_____

_____

Case B

Haddie and Lester's job is to measure the places where streets will be built. They record how steep hills are, and how much space is available for the street. They also record anything that stands out about the area. With these measurements, construction crews will know exactly where to put the street. Haddie and Lester must work in all kinds of weather. Suppose that Haddie and Lester work more slowly one day because it is raining very hard. They feel worried that they will not make it to every location that they must measure. Name one thing Haddie and Lester could do that would help them finish their work effectively.

_____

_____

Case C

Leroy is a legal secretary. He works for two lawyers. One day, Leroy is especially busy. He types a long document, prints it, and then runs to the printer and waits while it prints. He must mail the document to nine different attorneys. Leroy prepares each package one at a time. He types the cover letter, copies the cover letter and the document, and types a mailing label. Then, Leroy labels the envelope, stuffs the document and cover letter inside, and mails it. He goes through this process nine times, once for each lawyer he must mail the document to. It takes Leroy three hours to do this. In the meantime, the lawyers Leroy works for have been producing more work for him. Leroy has fallen behind in his other work while he prepared the documents to be mailed. How could Leroy have managed his time better?

_____

_____

TRY IT OUT

Interview someone from your community who often must manage time during a crisis. For example, you might interview an emergency medical technician, a firefighter, or a police officer. Or, you could interview a legal secretary, a plumber, a cook, or a youth division aide. Use your imagination. Ask how this person manages his or her time during a crisis. Then discuss what you learned with a small group. Discuss how the techniques used by the interview subjects could help you.

Think and Apply

How well do you use the skills in this lesson? Complete these exercises.

A. Think about what you learned in this lesson and answer the questions. Share your answers with your partner or your class.

1. When was the last time that you were in a crisis situation at work, school, or home? Explain what happened. How did you deal with the crisis?

   _____

   _____

2. During the next week, use breathing techniques for crises at work or at home. Breathe in and out slowly, at least three times, before you deal with the situation. Then explain how stopping to breathe affected the way you reacted to the crisis.

   _____

B. Review your answers to A. Complete the checklist. Then answer the questions that follow.

1. Read the list of skills. Check the boxes next to your strengths.
   - ☐ lowering stress
   - ☐ gathering information
   - ☐ listing pros and cons
   - ☐ rating your decisions
   - ☐ arranging the steps of each task in a faster order
   - ☐ grouping tasks together
   - ☐ using downtime
   - ☐ delegating work to coworkers

2. Do you want to improve any of your skills? Which ones?

   _____

3. How do you plan to improve the skills you listed in question 2?

   _____

Organizing Materials and Work Space

How do you organize your work space?

How does it help you get your work done?

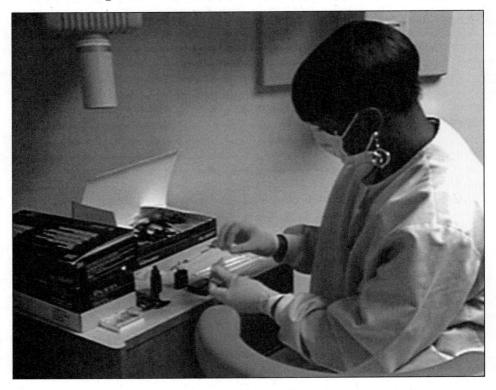

Arranging your materials in an orderly way will help save time.

Have you ever heard the saying, "An ounce of prevention is worth a pound of cure?" When you are organized, you are practicing prevention. You are preventing yourself from losing time. For example, the ten minutes it takes you to look for a power drill or a customer's phone number is ten minutes you have wasted. Being **organized** means that you can find materials quickly. It also means that you have arranged your work space to help you work better. You can get to everything you need efficiently. **Efficiency** means working well without wasting time or effort. If your work space is organized efficiently, you can spend more time on-task. To be **on-task** means to actually do your job, instead of getting ready to do it.

Organize Tools and Materials

One of the first tasks you should do for any job is to get your materials and tools ready. You should collect materials ahead of time. Place your tools within reach. For example, workers who build electronic devices should place electronic parts and tools near their work area. Bakers should make sure that a rolling pin and knife are stored within reach of the table where they knead the dough.

Set Up a Filing System

Looking for a piece of paper wastes time. To organize papers and documents so you can find them later, sort them according to **categories,** or subjects. Some offices have their own **filing system,** a specific way of categorizing and filing papers. However, you can make up your own filing system at home and on some jobs. You might file folders in alphabetical order. Your system should make sense to you and be easy to remember. When you organize files, you are also being respectful of your coworkers. Your coworkers must be able to find documents in files that you share. They must also be able to find documents in your files when you are on vacation or are out sick.

Having the necessary tools and materials within reach can save you time.

Even if you do not work with paper, a filing system can help you. You may have to keep track of supplies. Construction workers need a system for keeping track of nails, drill bits, and screws. Restaurant workers need a system for keeping track of dry ingredients that are stored on shelves, and a system for keeping track of ingredients that must be kept cool, in a refrigerator or freezer. These items might be alphabetized, or they might be stored according to how often they are used. Food may be stored from oldest to freshest.

Respond to Incoming Documents Promptly

An **in-box** is a tray for gathering incoming papers and documents you need to read. Don't put a paper back in your in-box after you have read it. Instead, decide what to do with it. If the paper calls for action soon, put it in a "to-do" pile. You may have a "to-do-today" pile for work you must do now and a "to-do" pile for things that can wait a day or two. Papers that you will need later should be filed right away in the correct file. Everything else should be recycled or thrown away.

Use Technology to Help You Organize

Documents are handled on a computer the same way that paper documents are handled. Most computer software programs arrange information in "files." Your computer's memory is like a large filing cabinet. A sales representative might keep a **database,** or set of information stored on a computer, to record the types of products each customer usually buys and how much each customer usually spends. The sales representative can search her database to find out which customers might be interested in a particular product. The following case study shows how a dental assistant uses technology.

Case Study

Elissa is a dental assistant. Every morning Elissa checks to make sure there are plenty of materials in the dentist's examining rooms. She sterilizes the instruments. Elissa keeps a database that has information about patients. Before she sees a patient, Elissa looks the patient up in her database. Her database tells her when the patient last had an X ray. Elissa uses this information to determine whether the patient needs an X ray on this visit or not.

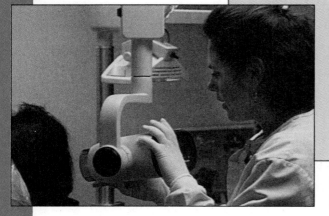

In medical offices, workers use technology to provide health care for patients.

Elissa's methods help her do a good job. When she is with a patient, the materials she needs are right at hand. If the patient needs an X ray, Elissa takes it right away. She develops the X ray while the dentist examines the patient. By doing this, Elissa saves time for herself, the dentist, and the patient.

Customize Your Work Space

You will probably have to adjust your work space to suit your own needs. When you do this, you are **customizing** your work space. In the following case study, a childcare aide helps arrange the classroom into several small areas.

Case Study

Brenda, a childcare aide, makes the most of space in her workplace. She has helped arrange the classroom so it is efficient and safe. Brenda put books and toys on the lower shelves within easy reach of the children. This saves time because the children don't have to ask a staff member to get things down. She stored items for the staff on higher shelves. Other activities take place in different areas in the room. For example, the painting table is separated from other areas by low shelves that hold aprons and cleaning supplies. Brenda can use these materials to clean up very quickly after an art class. The area where students meet to hear stories has a soft, comfortable rug to sit on. Because students sit on the floor for story time, Brenda does not lose time arranging chairs.

No matter what you do or where you do it, take time "up front" to set up the space, organize your tasks, and arrange your tools. Don't hesitate to experiment with different setups until you find one that's right. The less time it takes to reach materials and tools, the more time you can spend on-task. The result will be more time for the job and for yourself.

Comprehension Check

Complete the following exercises. Refer to the lesson if necessary.

A. Name one way you can sort papers from your in-box.

_____

_____

B. What are three possible decisions you could make about each paper or document you have to deal with?

1. _____

2. _____

3. _____

C. Mark the following statements T (True) or F (False).

_____ 1. Organizing your work space saves you time in the long run because it prevents you from losing materials that you will need later.

_____ 2. Organizing your files saves you time, but it does not help other people.

_____ 3. The best way to use your in-box is to hold only papers that you have not yet read.

_____ 4. Being efficient means learning from mistakes.

_____ 5. In a filing system, paper is sorted by category.

_____ 6. You can use the same system to organize computer files that you would use to organize paper files.

_____ 7. To be on-task means to be doing your job.

_____ 8. Papers that you might need to review right away should be filed in your "to-do-today" pile.

Making Connections

Answer the questions following each case. Then talk about your answers with your partner or group.

Case A

Michael sells fancy pens and pencils to office supply and large department stores. Michael works from an office in his home. He keeps track of about one hundred current customers and fifty potential customers. He also tries to contact new stores. He keeps samples and displays of the pens and pencils so that he is ready to show them to new customers. He also sends information to his customers about new products. He takes customer orders that are later filled by a central warehouse. The warehouse lets him know when the orders are shipped.

Name one way that being organized helps Michael save time.

_____

_____

_____

_____

_____

_____

Case B

Diane is an insurance underwriter for HealthCare USA. She has asked Imelda to file the following papers. Imelda has a legal file, a company documents file, a financial file, an industry information file, and a card file.

1. The minutes from Diane's last department meeting
2. A business trip hotel bill
3. A document from Susan Straw's lawsuit against HealthCare USA
4. A business card for Callahan, Attorney at Law
5. A newsletter—the most recent copy of *Insurance Law Today*
6. A bill from Callahan, Attorney at Law

7. Several legal forms
8. A business lunch receipt
9. A business card for Acme Insurance
10. A copy of an article, "Insurance Underwriters in the 90s"
11. HealthCare USA's retirement plan
12. HealthCare USA's employee manual
13. A message from a client with a phone number that Diane needs
14. Several expense report forms

1. What documents go in the legal file? Write the numbers.

   _____

2. What documents go in the company documents file?

   _____

3. What documents should Imelda put in the financial file?

   _____

4. What documents go in the industry information file?

   _____

5. What documents should go in her card file?

   _____

TRY IT OUT

Meet with a group of two or three classmates. Each of you volunteer to interview a worker in your community. State what type of worker you plan to interview. Make sure that each of you will interview a worker who does a different job. Interview the worker. Ask how she or he organizes his or her work space. Ask how being organized helps the worker save time. Then, meet again with your group. Share what you learned.

Think and Apply

How well do you use the skills in this lesson? Complete these exercises.

A. Think about what you learned in this lesson and answer the questions. Share your answers with your partner or your class.

1. How do you organize your jobs or projects? Do you think about order or sequence of tasks? Give an example of a large task that you broke into smaller tasks.

    _____

2. Describe how you organize all your important papers including mail, school information, and personal papers like birth certificates and leases. How might you improve your organization?

    _____

3. List some ways you could improve your work space. You may want to make a diagram to show how your space would be redesigned.

    _____

B. Review your answers to A. Complete the checklist. Then answer the questions that follow.

1. Read the list of skills. Check the boxes next to your strengths.

    ☐ organizing tools and materials

    ☐ filing

    ☐ responding to incoming documents

    ☐ using appropriate technology to help with organizing

    ☐ customizing shared work space

2. Do you want to improve any of your skills? Which ones?

    _____

3. How do you plan to improve the skills you listed in question 2?

    _____

Avoiding Time Wasters

What situations waste your time at work?

How do you organize yourself to handle them better?

Identify and avoid time wasters to get the most from your day.

To save time, you must avoid wasting time. This sounds easy, but it can be difficult. First, identify the time wasters in your day. Some time wasters result from a lack of organization. Others come from handling personal business at work. Second, when you see a time waster coming toward you, take action to avoid it. Don't fall into the trap of wasting time.

Think Ahead

Thinking ahead can prevent you from losing time. Suppose you are close to finishing an important task. Then you discover that you are missing something that you need to complete the job. This is like a mechanic taking the old fan belt out of a car, and then finding that he doesn't have a new one to replace it. Before you begin a task, gather the materials that you will need.

At other times you may think you have completed a task, only to discover that it must be redone. This can happen if you don't ask questions. This might mean only a minor loss of time. Or it might mean repeating several steps in your work. Read the following case study. Notice how Teresa loses time because she does not ask an important question.

To avoid wasting time, make sure you understand job tasks that involve several steps.

Case Study

Teresa must design the window display for a clothing store. Her supervisor, Jerome, has asked Teresa to design something that will show off the new spring merchandise. Teresa wonders whether Jerome intends for the display to show off the new spring dresses or the new bathing suits. Teresa decides to just go ahead. She designs a display for the bathing suits. When Jerome sees it, he is quite surprised. He expected her to display the new spring dresses. Teresa must redo all of her work.

Limit Your Personal Time

Personal time on the job means everything from time taken for breaks and lunch to time spent in personal phone conversations or chatting with coworkers. Many employers set strict limits to personal time. For example, receiving personal phone calls may not be allowed except in emergencies. Or personal calls may be permitted only during your break time or for just a few minutes.

Employer expectations vary from job to job. Some jobs require employees to talk together to find solutions to problems in the workplace. If you work in this type of position, be sure to limit your conversation. Discuss only the problem that needs to be solved. Don't get sidetracked into discussing your personal life with your coworkers. If you like your coworkers, you can work together more productively as a team. But if you want to talk to them about nonwork matters, do it on your breaks, at lunch, or after work, as shown in the following case study.

Case Study

Sharon is a counselor for a social service agency. She must answer hotline calls and talk with walk-in clients. Sharon uses the time in between phone calls and visits from walk-in clients to catch up on paperwork. Four other counselors share an office and files with Sharon. The counselors often must discuss clients with each other. But Sharon is careful not to waste time talking about other matters.

Elena: I don't know how to help my client, Susanna. She only speaks Ukrainian.

Sharon: Did you know that Olga speaks Ukrainian? She can translate for you.

Elena: I didn't know that! Thank you, I'll call her. By the way, did you watch the game last night?

Sharon: Oh yes, I did. Wasn't it exciting! Let's talk at lunch.

Remember to be friendly to coworkers but also careful not to waste their time talking about personal matters.

Sharon responds with enthusiasm to Elena's mention of the game. But she does not allow her enthusiasm to distract her from her work. Sharon shows that she respects her own time and Elena's time by scheduling a time when they can talk about the game outside of work.

Don't Spin Your Wheels

You can also lose time when working on your own. You may reach a point in your work where you need to ask a coworker or supervisor for help. Gather as much information as you can, and try to move forward. If you are "blocked" on one project, put it aside and try to proceed on another. You may find that when you return to the first task, it will be easier to find a solution.

Value Other People's Time

You must avoid wasting your coworkers' time as well as your own. One way to do this is to limit the time you spend discussing personal subjects with them. Another way is to double-check your work and correct errors before they spread and affect other people's work.

Also, sometimes you may have to ask a coworker for instructions, information, or materials. Organize yourself before you talk to your coworker. Make sure you know what you need. Ask all your questions at once. Don't ask one question, walk away, and then come back and interrupt your coworker a second time.

On occasion you may be involved in meetings. Come prepared to participate actively in a discussion. However, don't talk about issues not related to the meeting.

Check Your Progress

To see whether you are wasting time, check your progress. Review your plans, the tasks you have carried out, and the results you have achieved. Notice whether you are likely to fall behind by the end of the day, week, or month. If you think that you will not be able to finish, think about ways you can avoid wasting time.

Recognize the factors that often waste your time. Otherwise, you will always feel like you are behind. If you identify time wasters and avoid them, you will accomplish more at work.

Comprehension Check

Complete the following exercises. Refer to the lesson if necessary.

A. How can you avoid getting involved in a task and then finding out you are missing an important tool, material, or piece of information?

_____

_____

B. What should you avoid talking about during meetings?

_____

_____

C. Complete the following sentences. Circle the letter in front of the answer.

1. To avoid time wasters, you must
    a. refuse to talk to coworkers.
    b. not take time making lists.
    c. recognize them promptly.

2. A good example of limiting your personal time at the job is
    a. skipping lunch.
    b. keeping to yourself.
    c. limiting personal phone calls to a few minutes.

3. A worker who wants to save time
    a. can't be bothered with organizing his or her tools.
    b. values others' time as well as his or her own.
    c. thinks first of his or her own time sheet.

4. If you feel blocked on a task, a good approach is to
    a. put it aside for a while and take care of something else.
    b. tell your supervisor you can't do the job.
    c. dig in your heels and try again.

Making Connections

Answer the questions following each case. Then talk about your answers with your partner or group.

Case A

Jeff works in the admissions office of a large hospital. He is responsible for showing patients to their rooms and taking care of various office tasks like typing and filing. Over the last two weeks he also has been training a new employee. As a result, he has not done the filing. Now there is a big stack of reports and letters on his desk that need to be filed, and it's almost the end of his shift. He wonders where all the time has gone.

Then Jeff's supervisor comes into the room and tells him, "I'd like you to take care of that filing tomorrow." Jeff knows his supervisor expects him to catch up on the filing right away, but he isn't sure he's going to have the time.

How could Jeff have prevented this situation?

_____

_____

Case B

Al has a job delivering snack foods to customers with vending machines. He is expected to make ten deliveries a day, to sites located far apart from each other in the city. He enjoys chatting with his customers and building relationships with them. Recently, however, the traffic has been heavier on the roads he takes. He only manages to make seven of the ten deliveries each day.

What changes can Al make to his work habits so he will have time to do all ten deliveries?

_____

_____

Case C

Cory is a receptionist at a dental office. She starts work at eight o'clock. Today she needs to call five people to confirm appointments. Then she needs to pull their charts to prepare for the dentist to see them. In addition, she needs to file last week's charts and input the billing.

In the morning, she calls the five people. They are not there, so she leaves messages. Then she begins the filing. By the time she finishes, four of the five people have called back and she has set up their appointments. Now she can begin pulling their charts for the dentist.

What problem has Cory avoided by making the calls first?

_____

_____

TRY IT OUT

Visit a business in your community. Interview the manager. Ask the manager to tell you the three biggest time wasters that he or she has observed. Then, share what you have learned with your classmates.

Think and Apply

How well do you use the skills in this lesson? Complete these exercises.

A. Think about what you learned in this lesson and answer the questions. Share your answers with your partner or your class.

1. When was the last time you thought you wasted time at work or at school? Describe the situation. What could you have done differently?

   _____

   _____

2. Think of one task you would like to accomplish. It can be a work task or personal task. Think ahead. How can you accomplish this task?

   _____

   _____

B. Review your answers to A. Complete the checklist. Then answer the questions that follow.

1. Read the list of skills. Check the boxes next to your strengths.
   - ☐ thinking ahead
   - ☐ limiting personal time
   - ☐ valuing other people's time
   - ☐ avoiding the problem of "spinning my wheels"
   - ☐ checking my progress

2. Do you want to improve any of your skills? Which ones?

   _____

   _____

3. How do you plan to improve the skills you listed in question 2?

   _____

   _____

Check What You've Learned will give you an idea of how well you've learned about the time management skills you'll need to use in the workplace.

Read each question. Circle the letter before the answer.

1. Janet works as a secretary in a museum. She has been assigned to help develop a policy manual for employees. Janet doesn't know where to start. She should

   a. request a different assignment.
   b. wait and hope that her task will get simpler.
   c. break the assignment down into steps.

2. Stan is a waiter in a restaurant. During meal times, there are many customers, and the restaurant is noisy. What should Stan pay attention to while he is taking an order from a customer?

   a. The cook who announces which meals are ready to be served.
   b. Other waiters who are discussing their plans for the weekend.
   c. The customer's question about what the dessert specials are.

3. Nate is reorganizing the files at an insurance company. Which task is the most important for him to remember?

   a. He should finish the filing in the least possible time.
   b. He should file everything where others can also find it.
   c. He should file everything where he can find it.

4. Linda is a supervisor in a printing company. Part of her work involves writing memos to other employees. Recently Linda found out that she is not getting prompt responses to several of her memos, but she is not sure which ones still need to be answered. What does Linda need to do to be sure she doesn't forget about the memos that haven't gotten responses yet?

   a. use a tickler file
   b. meet deadlines
   c. be considerate of other people's time

5. Penny works as a youth counselor. She is especially busy during the summer. Penny finds many of the problems these young people bring to her very disturbing. Lately Penny has had some trouble sleeping. What does Penny need to do?

   a. group her appointments together
   b. reduce stress
   c. figure out why she procrastinates

6. Lisa is a travel agent. Recently her supervisor told Lisa that she needs to limit her personal time on the job. Which of these things should Lisa do?

   a. She should skip lunch.
   b. She should avoid talking to anyone else on the job.
   c. She should limit making or receiving personal phone calls at work.

7. John is an account manager in a mailing house. He is facing several deadlines now. If he had gotten a quicker start on some of these projects, he would be under less pressure. What does John need to learn how to do better?

   a. delegate work to coworkers
   b. figure out why he procrastinates
   c. value other people's time

8. Greg is part of a work team at a meat packing company. Recently the team has found that several of its projects have taken more time than expected. Greg is now conducting a review of its work. What would he most likely conclude?

   a. The team did not estimate correctly how much time each task would require.
   b. The team did not identify its goals.
   c. The team did not meet its deadlines.

9. Isabel is an administrative assistant. She is good at responding to daily problems. However, she has not been making any progress on longer-term projects. Isabel needs to

a. work more carefully.

b. ignore the problems.

c. resolve the conflicts between her long- and short-term assignments.

10. Amanda works in a college admissions office. She writes reminders to herself on small pieces of paper. Now she has 45 such reminders pinned to her bulletin board. What is the main problem with this approach?

a. Too many notes makes it hard to see the priorities.

b. The notes are too small for her to write down all the details.

c. The notes will distract her from her work.

Review Chart

The chart below shows you which skills you need to study. Reread each question you missed. Then look at the appropriate lesson of the book for help in understanding the correct answer.

Question Check the questions you missed.	**Skill** The exercise, like the book, focuses on the skills below.	**Lesson** Review what you learned in this book.
1. _____	Breaking a task into steps	1
2. _____	Focusing on your job	4
3. _____	Organizing materials	9
4. _____	Keeping a tickler file	7
5. _____	Reducing stress	8
6. _____	Limiting personal time at work	10
7. _____	Preventing procrastination	6
8. _____	Estimating time	2
9. _____	Handling assignments	3
10. _____	Keeping track of priorities	5

Glossary

analyze: To study a problem by carefully examining its parts. page 5

assignment: Something given as a task or amount of work. page 5

calendar: A table arranged to show time in years, months, weeks, and days. page 54

card file: A tool that is used to keep track of names, addresses, and phone numbers. page 55

categories: Divisions or groups used to organize something. page 69

communicate: To exchange information. page 14

crisis: An emergency. page 60

customizing: Adjusting or changing according to individual needs. page 71

database: A set or collection of information stored on a computer. page 70

deadline: The date or time that you must finish by. page 54

delegating: Giving duties or work to another person. page 63

distractions: Things that get your attention but are not related to your work. page 28

downtime: The time when a machine or person is inactive. page 62

effective: Getting the wanted result. page 62

efficiently: Without waste. page 68

equipment: Machines and other things that help people do their work. page 13

estimate: A guess about how much time or money something will take. page 14

false start: An unsuccessful attempt to begin a project or goal. page 12

filing system: A specific way of organizing papers and documents so they are easy to find. page 69

flexible: Being able to change as situations change. Adaptable. page 39

in-box: A tray for people to put incoming papers and documents for you to read. page 70

long-term goals: Needs and wants that extend into the future for long periods of time. Career planning is an example of a long-term goal. page 20

materials: Objects and items necessary for making or doing something. page 13

motivation: The reason that causes a person to act. page 46

on task: Refers to time spent focused on a particular piece of work rather than doing something else. page 68

organized: Arranged or ordered. page 68

personal time: Time taken away from work for breaks, lunch, and personal phone calls, or chatting with coworkers. page 77

priorities: Tasks listed in order of importance. pages 6, 36

procrastination: The act of putting off action until a future time. page 44

reference: A source of information, such as a map, telephone book, or dictionary. page 55

resources: Supplies or talents (equipment, materials, people) needed to complete a project or task. pages 21, 38

routine: A fixed way of doing something. page 55

schedule: A time table showing when work tasks will occur and how long they will take. page 54

self-starter: Someone who begins or gets projects started without being told. page 46

sequencing: Arranging steps in the order that you do them. page 6

short-term goals: Needs and wants that extend for short periods of time. page 20

tickler file: A file where you can keep a reminder to do certain tasks. page 54

time sheet: A record of the amount of time spent on each work task. page 31

to-do list: A list of all the tasks you need to do. page 54

trade-off: Giving up one goal in favor of another. page 23

urgent: Needing or requiring attention or action right away. page 22

visualize: To imagine or make a picture in your mind. page 14

Answer Key

For many exercises in this book, several answers are possible. You may want to share your answers with your teacher or another learner.

Check What You Know (pages 1–3)

1. b	2. c	3. b	4. b
5. a	6. a	7. b	8. b
9. c	10. c		

Lesson 1

Comprehension Check (page 8)

A. Analyzing makes it easier to set goals because when you analyze a large assignment, you can break it into smaller assignments.

B. An assignment is work that someone gives you. Finishing the assignment can be a goal. Workers often set their own goals to help them complete assignments.

C. 1. (c)   2. (b)   3. (a)   4. (c)

Making Connections (pages 9–10)

Case A

First: corrects homework
Second: helps make lesson plans for a history class
Third: puts up a display about the history lesson
Fourth: copies worksheets for students to do over the weekend

Case B

1. seating customers who are waiting for a table that has become available
2. operating the cash register for customers who are ready to pay for their meals and leave
3. helping to clear tables so that more customers can be seated
4. telling jokes to children in line

Case C

1. Cleaning computers on display, unloading boxes of CD-ROMs, and moving color printers
2. He forgot to move the printers.

3. Answers may include that Darryl could set goals and perhaps write them down.

Lesson 2

Comprehension Check (page 16)

A. Answers may include the following: make a plan that can help you avoid false starts, determine the best way of doing something, and think of ways to avoid problems before they occur.

B. Answers may include analyzing, visualizing, estimating, checking your progress, communicating, making a schedule, and reviewing.

C. 1. (a)   2. (c)   3. (c)   4. (b)

Making Connections (pages 17–18)

Case A

Gather material and equipment; use estimates and a calendar.

Case B

Answers will vary. The dispatcher should plan the work requests according to location. Based on estimated time required, the dispatcher should divide the work requests equally among the plumbers on duty if possible. The dispatcher might use the map and addresses to plan routes for each of the plumbers.

Case C

Answers will vary. Odessa can use the information about what days students would be able to attend class to choose what days she will teach. She can use the information about how much dance experience each student has to plan what dance steps she will teach in each class.

Lesson 3

Comprehension Check (page 24)

A. Answers may include that long-term goals are more complex and take longer than short-term goals.

B. 1. Finding out your own interests, abilities, values and goals, needs and wants
   2. Gather information about a career that fits what you find out about yourself.
   3. Choose a career goal and make a plan for achieving it.
C. 1. (c)   2. (b)   3. (c)   4. (a)

Making Connections (pages 25–26)

Case A
   Answers may include advertising in newspapers and running promotions to attract customers.

Case B
   Erin has a short-term goal to produce more parts per day. Sam and Connie also have short-term goals to produce more parts per week. The team has a long-term goal to complete eighty motors in two months.

Case C
   long-term goal, short-term goal, long-term goal, long-term goal, short-term goal, short-term goal

Lesson 4

Comprehension Check (page 32)

A. excess noise, frequent interruptions, poor work spaces, other employees, outside worries, and having too much work to do
B. You should concentrate on your work and not let irrelevant distractions bother you. But you should be alert to changing conditions that can affect your work.
C. 1. (a)   2. (b)   3. (a)   4. (a)

Making Connections (pages 33–34)

Case A
   1. She had too much work. She could not focus on a single task.
   2. She realized she could not complete the work by the end of the week. She asked for a meeting to figure out a way to finish the work.

Case B
   1. Dan told George that he'd like to hear George's ideas.
   2. Dan told George that right now was not a good time to talk. Dan said he had to focus on his deadline.

Lesson 5

Comprehension Check (page 40)

A. Answers may include finding out the deadline for each assignment, figuring out how long it will take to do each assignment, looking at the assignment from your employer's point of view, asking your supervisor, and deciding whether there is an emergency.
B. 1. priority   5. priorities
   2. resources   6. emergency
   3. flexible   7. point of view
   4. coworkers   8. supervisor

Making Connections (pages 41–42)

Case A
   Answers may include that Jo's priorities should change because needs have changed. A patient who is in pain should be more of a priority than a bed that needs to be made.

Case B
   1. Answers may include that Margo's priorities changed because her coworker, Tyrone, was out sick.
   2. Answers may include Margo responded to the change by adjusting her schedule and making time to do some of Tyrone's work.

Case C
   1. an emergency
   2. She is flexible. She rearranges her schedule.

Lesson 6

Comprehension Check (page 48)

A. Answers may include the following: they have run out of energy, they do not know where to start, they do not like to do a particular task, they are afraid to do a particular task, or they are in the habit of procrastinating.

B. Answers may include the following: keep a positive attitude or mix up work tasks.
C. 1. F   2. T   3. T
D. 1. (b)   2. (a)

Making Connections (pages 49–50)

Case A

1. Answers may include that Carmen puts off moving the plants because she is afraid of making a mistake.
2. Answers may include that she practices moving the plants until she is good at it. Then she will not have to worry so much. Carmen could also ask her supervisor to show her ways to be more careful when she moves the plants. Students may also suggest that Carmen should keep a positive attitude. This is an opportunity for her to learn.

Case B

1. Answers may include that Kenny puts off checking the equipment because he doesn't know where to start.
2. Answers may include that Kenny should change his habits. He could break the task into small steps and do a little each day.

Case C

1. Answers may include that Paulette puts off computer work because she is too tired to do it.
2. Answers may include that Paulette could change her schedule so that she does computer entry first thing in the morning, when she feels awake.

Lesson 7

Comprehension Check (page 56)

A. Answers may include: a calendar, a to-do list, a schedule, a tickler file, and references.
B. Answers may include: check your to-do list when you get to work, update your schedule for the day, group like activities together, stick to your to-do list, change your schedule if you are interrupted, and make your to-do list for the next day.

C. 1. (c)   2. (a)   3. (b)   4. (e)
    5. (d)   6. (f)   7. (g)

Making Connections (pages 57–58)

Case A

Answers may include that Maureen should follow a routine to help her stay on track. She should have checked the cargo in her truck before leaving. She should have checked her route. She should also have checked to see how much gas she had.

Case B

Answers may include David uses a calendar and a map.

Case C

Answers may include that Bill should check the Express-O schedules and routes to find out the fastest way to get the package to Houston. After he chooses a route, he should check the weather maps to make sure that the package will not be delayed by bad weather.

Lesson 8

Comprehension Check (page 64)

A. Answers may include taking time to breathe slowly, doing one thing at a time, handling your emotions, and taking action.
B. Downtime is any time when work is getting done, but you are not doing it. During that time, you can do something else.
C. 1. stress
    2. crisis
    3. courage
    4. information
    5. delegating
    6. group tasks
    7. pros and cons

Making Connections (pages 65–66)

Case A

Answers may include that Peter should stop and take a deep breath, that he should prioritize his tasks and help the sick passenger first. Peter could also ask

Vanessa for help, since making the announcement will only take her a few seconds. Peter could also save time by going to help the passengers and then distributing drinks on the way back.

Case B
Answers may include Haddie and Lester could order and group tasks. They might divide their grouped tasks or "delegate" to one another. They could do all the streets on one side of town first, and then measure streets on the other side of town.

Case C
Leroy should have used the downtime from printing to do something else. He also should have grouped like tasks together. He could have produced his cover letters in a batch, made his copies in a batch, typed his mailing labels in a batch, and then done all his envelope stuffing at once. This would have saved him eight trips back and forth to the copier, and eight trips back and forth to the printer.

Lesson 9

Comprehension Check (page 72)
A. Answers may include a to-do pile and a to-do-today pile.
B. Answers may include: put it in a to-do pile for action now; file it for later use; recycle it.
C. 1. T   2. F   3. T   4. F
   5. T   6. T   7. T   8. T

Making Connections (pages 73–74)
Case A
Answers may include when new customers come in, Michael is ready for them. He doesn't have to look for his samples. Customers have some idea what they want when they come in because Michael has sent them information about new products. Because the warehouse lets Michael know when orders are shipped, he can contact the customer if there is a problem.

Case B
1. 3, 7   2. 1, 11, 12
3. 2, 6, 8, 14   4. 5, 10
5. 4, 9, 13

Lesson 10

Comprehension Check (page 80)
A. Plan ahead and make sure that all necessary items and information are gathered before beginning the task.
B. Subjects unrelated to the meeting.
C. 1. (c)   2. (c)   3. (b)   4. (a)

Making Connections (pages 81–82)
Case A
Answers may include Jeff could have thought ahead and planned to do a little filing every day. He also could have checked his progress and learned that he was falling behind sooner.

Case B
Answers may include he could limit his personal time and spend less time chatting to store employees. He could also plan his route more carefully, so he visits all the stores in one part of town before delivering to stores in another part of town.

Case C
Answers may include that Cory has avoided spinning her wheels. She planned her time by trying to confirm the appointments first, and when she couldn't finish that, she switched to another task, the filing.

Check What You've Learned (pages 84–86)
1. c   2. c   3. b   4. a
5. b   6. c   7. b   8. a
9. c   10. a